Julian:

The Apple of My Eye!

Written by Cherry Carl

Images: art4crafts.com

Dedicated to Lisa and the staff
at the Julian Hotel
EST. 1897

to my loving husband,
who shared endless days and nights in Julian.

C.C.

Contents

Contents cont.

Preface

Julian, California, has always been one of my favorite places in the entire world. I came to the mountains in Southern California with my family when I was a young child, making trips as an adult with my own family and friends. We always stayed at the Julian Gold Rush Hotel and loved every peaceful moment spent there. That feeling has continued for over 70 years! Somehow, though, I am always moved to write something about the essence of this experience. Hence, this collection of Julian's gems.

Homecoming

The owner's daughter has a smile on her face,

As she opens the door to this peaceful place.

Our lovely room has a big brass bed,

And feather pillows to rest our heads.

The antique furnishings tell stories of old,

In this beautiful inn worth its weight in gold.

The noise of the tourists getting apple pie,

Ends for the day as night draws nigh.

No matter where we wander or roam,

Coming here is like coming home!

What Do I Do?

What do I do in the old hotel?

(It's not a fancy mod motel.)

There's not a T.V in every room.

(No telephone, you can presume!)

It's just a quiet, peaceful place,

With lots of lovely, tatted lace,

Books to read and games to play,

A rocking chair to sit and stay.

A fire warms my heart and soul,

And a happy hearth makes me whole!

Come to the Mountains!

Come to the mountains and this tiny town,

The one that is dressed in nature's gown.

It's surrounded by curtains of tall, tall trees,

Their piney smell's perfume on the breeze!

Now and then you may spy a deer,

Or a tumble of turkeys,

With their call of good cheer!

They are all a very welcome sight,

From dawn's early morning,

To the evening's moonlight.

Boom Town!

Fetch the water from the brook,

Do the mending, clean and cook!

Find a skillet, bake a pie.

Earn some coins when miners buy!

Build a business, take your pick!

Our boom town's growing,

Quick, quick, quick!

Miners stopped to rest a spell,

And found our boom town's really swell!

Stables, stores, a schoolhouse, too,

That the way our boom town grew!

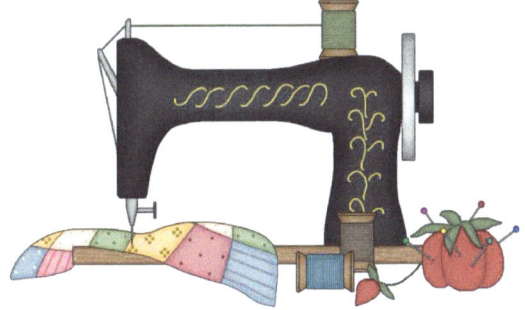

Grandma's Feather Bed

"Now I lay me down to sleep.
I pray the Lord my soul to keep."
This soft little prayer, word for word,
Is what our grandma always heard,
When she tucked us into the feather bed,
After our nightly prayers were said.

Dressed in flannel to keep out the cold,
We listened as Grandpa's stories were told.
Sometimes we'd have some cookies and milk,
Then cuddle with quilts as smooth as silk.
Sleeping in Grandma's feather bed,
Was the best place ever to lay my head.

There's comfort in memories of the past,
Of things that are gone and didn't last.
Julian has that same appeal.
When we spend the night and have a meal.
There's one thing missing that I forgot,
But you can have the chamber pot!

First Snow

The night is dark, clouds fill the sky.

We listen to the wind with its wail and its cry,

As the raging storm of rain and sleet,

Pounds on the roof with its giant feet.

As we watch from the window,

The sleet turns to slush.

The wailing winds have been told to hush.

We watch as a change comes over the sky.

Listen to the wind, now a whispery sigh,

As the silent storm, with its flakes of snow,

Walks on the roof with an angel's toe.

Needle and Thread

Grandma worked wonders with needle and thread,
As she stitched in the lamplight on the old homestead.
She'd sit right down in her rickety old chair,
And cut out colorful quilting squares.
There was Daddy's favorite threadbare shirt,
And dresses from his sisters and Grandma's skirt.
Each patch told a story of life long ago,
As memories were saved within each row.
These scraps of life became a cozy quilt,
A quilt that would last with colors that wilt.
That lovely old quilt kept us nice and warm.
Through many a night of a thunderous storm,
Grandma's quilt was a sweet caress,
As she said good night and, "May God bless."
We were two little girls, such sleepyheads,
Warmed by her love on the old homestead.

Winter Wonderland

We woke up today to a world of white!

Look what happened overnight!

We'll be outside with the first sunlight.

It's time to win a snowball fight!

We'll slide down the hill and come to a stop,

Right in a snowdrift! Oh! Kerplop!

We'll build a snowman, a scarf at his throat,

And don't forget his overcoat!

We stopped to look at the darkening sky.

"Let's go in for apple pie!"

We'd better watch the weather forecast,

To see if this wonderland will last!

Christmas in Julian

We let our Christmas Eve begin,
At the Julian hotel, a welcoming inn,
A perfect place with warmth to share,
With all who come from here and there,
A big brass bed with a cozy quilt,
That loving hands of yore have built,
Afternoon tea with goodies galore,
Scones and jam and muffins and more!
Yes, we let our Christmas morn begin,
At the Julian Hotel, that welcoming inn,
A Christmas tree with ribbons of light,
Makes the lobby so festive and bright.
We sit together and eagerly await,
The breakfast fare so we won't be late!
We've come to Julian, the place on the hill,
And we'll return. We know we will!

The Feathered Nest

It's just a little cabin sitting high on a hill,
But it's our little love nest among the whippoorwill.
Birds learn from Mother Nature,
To find the perfect spot,
So we learned from their lessons,
And here's what we got!
It's high among the trees and strong as an oak.
It's protected from the winds,
And the snow and the smoke,
Of other feathered nests on Salton Vista Drive,
So here we will stay and grow and thrive!
It's warm and cozy and safer than the rest.
That's why we call it The Feathered Nest!

It's Time for Tea!

It's almost three and time for tea!
Let's meet in the parlor, just you and me!
My wind-blown hair is just a mess,
And there's no need for fancy dress.
We can wear jeans and tennis shoes,
Or any comfy clothes we choose.
Who cares about wind and snow and ice,
When there's tea and cookies full of spice?

Tea for Two

Let's share the day,
And have some tea.
Oh my, now can't you see?
There's enough for you and me!
Let's go and sit among the flowers,
And giggle and talk for hours and hours!
Tea for two will be such fun!
It's so much better than tea for one!

Treasures in a Trunk

What treasures hide within this trunk?
Is it full of wonders or a pile of junk?
Some mamas kept their precious things,
Even silly dime store rings,
A christening gown, a baby's shoe,
Faded photos, just a few.
There may be letters from a homesick kid,
With news of all the things she did,
All bits and pieces of childhood years,
That always remind us of laughs and tears.

Nameless Faces

I wander up and down the hall,

Looking at pictures that hang on the wall.

Who is this man in the weathered frame?

Does he even have a name?

Did he come in the days of old,

With the other miners looking for gold?

Who is the bride who stands at his side?

Can she be identified,

This lovely lady with the parasol,

Or is she meant to remain on the wall?

They survived the wind and the ice and the snow,

These nameless faces from long ago.

Faded Photographs

The faded photos of a woman's life,

Are tucked away inside an old book.

This pretty person, a mother and wife,

Saved them for someone to take a look.

What dreams are hidden behind the eyes,

Of the very young girl, so warm and wise?

What secret longings, what memories,

What silent sorrows and things that please?

We'll never know, but we can guess,

About the lovely lady in the lacy dress.

All Things Fall

A scarecrow dressed in overalls,

Is just one sign of coming fall.

He seems to wave at each haystack,

As blackbirds dive in their attack,

On cornfields picked so bare and clean,

Changed to brown from summer's green.

Someone's baking apple pies,

Bread dough's set aside to rise.

A barnyard's full of fresh picked corn,

Pecked by a cackling white leghorn.

Geese are flying overhead,

Above the trees of orange and red.

Springtime Sings!

Julian's green as green can be,
Or so it seems to be to me!
I hear and smell the springtime grow,
And see it in each new rainbow.
Bumblebees hum to butterflies,
While grasshoppers leap up to the skies.
Bluebirds build their nests above,
And lay their eggs with a Mother's love.
Anthills rise above the ground,
And ladybugs fly around and around.
The sunshine turns to skies of gray,
As a gentle rainstorm comes our way.
Splash in the puddles left from the rain!
Springtime sings her song again!

Fine Catch on the Lake!

One fine morning in spring, we're awake,

We head to Julian's nearby lake*.

The newness of daybreak glistens,

On the damp seats of our boat,

As we sit and watch and listen.

My wiggly worm reaching out,

Dives down to the depths of the lake,

And comes back with a prize.

"What a catch!"

*Cuyamaca Lake is just around the bend.

Spring Fever

(Tune: The Mulberry Bush)

I meant to do some work today,

But a blue bird sang in the apple tree.

A butterfly flitted across the field . . . and,

All the trees were calling me!

The wind went sighing over the land,

Tossing the grasses to and fro,

A rainbow stretched its colorful band,

So, what could I do but laugh and go!

Johnny Appleseed

Johnny, Johnny Appleseed,

Thought he saw a great big need.

He walked across the U.S.A.

Spreading seeds along the way.

Thanks to his amazing deed,

Trees began to grow with speed.

Apples, apples, everywhere,

Enough to feed and enough to share!

How Do You Eat Your Apples?

How do you eat your apples?
Baked in a pie, candied or caramel?
Oh, me, oh, my!
Do you eat your apples with sharp cheddar cheese,
Or baked in a strudel? Danke and please!
Dumplings are as sweet as apple chips.
Anything with apples can pass through my lips!
Apple fritters, cobbler, apple butter, too,
I can eat them all and how about you?

Have an Apple!

Have an apple, fresh and sweet.
Oh, my goodness, what a treat!
Slice it up to eat with cheese,
Or peanut butter, if you please.

Eat it baked or eat it fried,
Or try some chips that have been dried.
Apple butter's good on toast,
Their apple strudel makes me boast,
That Julian makes the very best!
It's so much better than the rest!

It's Apple Picking Time!

Grab your basket, make it quick!
Autumn's here. It's time to pick,
Apples that are green and red.
And ready for the pies ahead!
We have to pick them all by hand,
(Because they bruise, I understand.)
The sun and the rain and the busy bees,
Have done their work on the apple trees.
So pick a dozen, maybe two.
We'll bake some pies when we are through!

Winter's Coming!

Storm windows, flannel sheets,
Comfy quilts that can't be beat!
Firewood's waiting by the door,
And right out back we have lots more!
Don't forget to find the sled,
That's hanging in the barn or shed.
Dig out your boots before the snow.
We're off to town with kids in tow!

The Corner Store

Scarves and skirts and lots of them!

Jams and jellies and jewelry and gems.

Caramel apples and sweets to eat.

Oh, the treats on Julian's streets!

There's a corner store for every taste.

Look at them all, don't choose in haste!

(It's where I always buy my mittens!)

I do admit I'm really smitten,

With Julian's collection of corner stores,

And I will be back forevermore!

Everything Nice!

What is Julian made of?

Apple pies and mountain skies!

That's what Julian is made of!

What is Julian made of?

Friendly folks and chimney smoke!

That's what Julian is made of!

What is Julian made of?

Sugar and spice and everything nice!

That's what Julian is made of!

Love's Lullaby

We drive to Julian, my winter
sweet love and I,
To that peaceful place,
Where the earth meets the sky.
We shop and buy a thing or two,
And do the things that tourists do.
At the end of the day,
When we're full and fed,
The hotel beckons and we're off to bed.
As the soft and quiet sounds of the night,
Settle around us, things feel right.
The sound of silence surrounds us here,
And I'm lulled by the feeling of everything dear.

Sleep Well!

The day is done.

You've had such fun,

It's time to stop and rest a spell.

So, we say goodnight and may you sleep well!

www.ingramcontent.com/pod-product-compliance
Lightning Source LLC
Chambersburg PA
CBHW040849120626
46547CB00001B/97